CAMP WINAPOOKA

Poems

Scott Laudati

.Bone Machine, Inc.

CAMP WINAPOOKA Copyright © 2019 by Scott Laudati. All rights reserved. No part of this book may be used or reproduced in any manner whatsoever without written permission by publisher, except in case of brief quotations embodied in reviews, essays, podcasts, and journals.

First Edition

ISBN: 0-578-48736-5
ISBN-13: 978-0-578-48736-6

BONE MACHINE, INC.
14 Allen Avenue
Manasquan, NJ 08736

www.BoneMachineBooks.com
ReadBoneMachine@gmail.com

Edited by: Christina Hart

Printed in the United States of America

also by SCOTT LAUDATI

.poems.
Hawaiian Shirts In The Electric Chair
Bone House

.novel.
Play The Devil

DEDICATION

For five brothers I'm proud to have shared many fox holes with – Drew Alexander Ennis, Ben M., Joey B, Joe La, and Brian Weakly.

My beautiful Satine and my killer Drake.

Caitlin Burke for EVERYTHING else.

And Heather Heyer, an American martyr, the bravest of us all. Rest in peace.

TABLE OF CONTENTS

I. *LAPSARIAN FATIGUE*

MY FIRST NIGHT BACK	1
THE LAST STREETLIGHT IN HEAVEN	2
MY BLUEST VALENTINE	4
A PRETTY PLAGUE	5
WHAT WAS YOUR SIN?	8
FISH TANK	11
BLACK FRIDAY	12

II. *HOLLYWOOD HELL*

MY SUITCASE IS PACKED	15
NEW FRIENDS	16
GOODNIGHT MOON	19
THE SANTA FE TRAIL	21
WHAT'S ENOUGH?	23
MY 30TH BIRTHDAY	25

III. *CONTRIBUTIONS TO DELINQUENCY*

THE END OF THE NIGHT	29
WE'RE HALFWAY THERE	32
THE BLOOD MOONS	33
BEAUTIFUL THINGS	37
NIGHT BEFORE THANKSGIVING	39
JERSEY SHORE	41

IV. *SHAMAN HAMAN*

A POEM FOR SATINE: A GOOD BOXER	44
WHEN I LOOK TO THE WEST	49

FUN TIME AMERICA	51
2ND GRADE	52
THE DREAM IS OVER PT. I	54
THE DREAM IS OVER PT. II	55

V. *BITE THE DIRT*

THE EXPERIMENT FAILED	58
CASINO DE MONTREAL	61
GREEN EYED ASHKENAZI GIRL	63
JUST LIKE W.3RD AT MIDNIGHT	65
HEROES	68
FIRST HIT	71
YOUR BOTTOM LINE	73
#OCCUPY	75

VI. *YETI FUNERAL*

A PLACE FOR EVERYONE	83
SOMEDAY I'LL GET THIS RIGHT	85
LUCKY US	87
FIN DE SES JOURS à GRAND EST (6/18/2018)	89
THE CLOCK SET BACK	91

VII. *BOONDOCKED IN PERICO*

THE EXODUS	94
THE THRONE	96
MEN	97
THE FORCED ENCORE	101
CLAYTON, NM	103
MERCY ME	105

CAMP WINAPOOKA

I.

lapsarian fatigue

(written in new york, new york 2014-2016)

my first night back.

we were far apart once
but you can hear my heart now
in this chest.
and your hair used to itch
my skin if you didn't tuck it back
but you'll never hear about it again
because i left you once
and i learned
to miss everything -
coffee at sunset
and all-night sirens up and down
amsterdam
while the pit bulls howled at
newspapers blowing by like
white rabbits taunting them
in the night.
and the coffee fades while the rum kicks in
and all those sounds fade to the periphery
like a television in someone
else's apartment.
and your hair crawls across my chest
like the tiny arms of a friendly spider.
you always knew what you had
but it took me a little longer.
there's no escape in my forever now,
our bones can grow soft in peace.
and that future we always talked about
can't come soon enough.

the last streetlight in heaven.

heaven's filling up with diplomas
from a youth
waiting single file
on the will call line.
and they listen to the crows
circling overhead
who learned a verse back when
they nested above the schools.
"it doesn't look like verona
anymore," they say.
"there's a dirt pit
where the swimming pool was."

i hope the boys can use
their track marks
as road maps
and hold the hands of girls
who sold their final sacraments
on the newark streets.
where spring feels like december,
where glass clogs the gutter,
and no price is too high
for a whole generation to erase
some of its hunger.

these towns flood now
but the rains never come.
there are enough mothers' tears
to water the lawns.

and in every man's poverty
we can see
the origin of night.
the first syringe.
the absence of god.
we were a class once but nothing is left.
and there's no sky clear enough
for the lucky ones to
reckon under.

a whole history of past sins
built above
indian bones.
the interest keeps rising on
america's crimes.
our parents lined up to vote
and prayed
it would always stay the same,
but the hurricane comes
and the shattered glass
gets washed away,
and they keep signing up fresh faces
to take its place.

my bluest valentine.

don't bake me a birthday cake
this year.
let's go to wawa and
buy a carton
of our old cigarettes
and drive to the poconos,
to the mini golf
where we made dirty bets
around the windmill
and both of us got a rash
that night from the
heart-shaped hot tub.
or we can go back
to your parents' basement
with the wood paneled walls
and the one cold night
we slept under the heater
and you whispered,
"pretend it's aspen."
let's get married this time
like we swore we would at seventeen
when all we wanted
was to do drugs and fall in love
and we were still young enough
to be good at both.

a pretty plague.

this couch again.
waking up dry under plants surrendered.
a little thirsty still from
my walk home last night.
the long shift ahead of me but this time
it isn't so bad.
the sous-chef at dirty french
sees me stealing oysters
and shows me how to slide a knife in
and open
an oyster clean.
a warm night down ludlow street
but the sky is winter clear
and i can make out a single star
while i hike across two villages
and father demo square.

all the old jesters are out holding court,
clutching onto their corners
before bank of america and
dunkin' donuts put them
on one-way buses
with no stops before
albany or troy.
the rat king outside of katz's
sits still in his wheelchair
waiting for scraps of pastrami.
punjabi drivers plan sit-ins
and suicides

at the basement deli on houston.
the last bar light on the bowery
flickers out like a blinking ghost
and i'm thinking,
"where am i?
what was the point of this thing
that they sailed oceans for?"

won't you meet me at fanelli's?
i want to hear your cello grind
in the libra wind
before
the final last call.
and bob at the bar, the serbian prince,
he hates you.
he hates me too.
he loved this city when no fire trucks
came to the rescue.
but we came.
we saved the neighborhood
we can't afford to drink in.
you're about to make it special, though.
your guy's coming and you've got a coupon.
the bags are $50 and the stuff
is all right.

cutting lines in the fanelli's bathroom
on a urinal three hundred years old.
should we stop and
appreciate the history here?
what did george washington do

on this porcelain?
a fork in the road for all of history.
he went left
and saved the world.
i went the other way and
woke up with you
on that shitty williamsburg sand,
covered in slime with
a cold wind against our ears.
and if i could go back
i wouldn't change a thing
because this world
always deserves a good story.
and so many have fought in revolutions
but so few
have fallen in love.
and while i watched your lips
back away
from your teeth so a smile
could paint your face
i knew that nothing
they ever fought for
could mean more than that morning.

what was your sin?

what was your sin?
were you born poor on this end of america?
did you notice a new vein
while the traffic camera flashed and
your knuckles scraped against the asphalt?
palms always up so
the voodoo lady on the corner
could get a read.
she ran the grange once
but they lock her up now for
practicing without a permit.
a bum by the bodega saw
the arrest and said,
"they would've charged jesus christ
for a fishing license if it got
a dollar out of him."

she didn't care about their rules, though.
she saw her god in the exhaust
behind the city bus.

we watched from the fire escape
and hatian women
brought her sticks and frogs
they'd stolen from the pet store.
the voodoo lady boiled it all in a bucket
outside the crown fried chicken
and when it turned green
everyone stuck a straw in

and took a nice big gulp.
they had black incense smoking
and a cat
they were about to skin
when the cops taped off the street.
a fat one put his boot on the bucket
and tipped the potion over
and as the green slime swam
for the sidewalk cracks
every fly in new york
showed up for dinner.
the cops handcuffed the voodoo lady
and she said to them,
"i'm the last saint of harlem.
that used to mean something."

we tried to go back but never tried to grow up.
remember, your great-grandfather wasn't
thomas jefferson -
even with all those student loans
you'll never be one of them.
and don't tell anyone you have the
slave blood running through you;
give them your heart
and they'll still bury you
on the other side of the fence.

it's everything a fairy tale isn't.
those ivory keys were carved
from whales' teeth.
these were the lessons of our youth

but your fingers never mainlined
the right vibe.
you think your luck is all bad
but remember,
you can still watch the sunset,
and that car you bought held up pretty good
after you killed your boss
over a weekend shift.
did you look back at the cart-boy?
he doesn't mean it
but he can't help making a "peace sign"
at the worst times.

the real hero rides shotgun and
smiles at the geckos,
while the good people wash dishes
and load their rifles.
and remember,
when the call comes
the voodoo lady said
they'd try and write down your license plate.
so drive fast, it won't be long before
they go blind
from the sunset.
and eventually you'll look like a comet,
and they'll wonder
if you came out the other side.

fish tank.

i believed in everything
when i was twenty
except when you told me
your tree had been cursed.
the dow jones crashed that day
or maybe
it was before the end of all things,
back when we watched saddam's body double
drop through the floor
and the crowd cheered
as the noose tightened.
we didn't look away from the computer screen
and i don't think i did again
until your mom showed up and
dumped my fish tank
full of fancy guppies down the toilet.
you packed your ysl heels back in the box
while i yelled at your mom
and no one listened
as i explained how hard it had been
to get those fish to breed.
no one listened at the bar that night either.
and i guess you were right,
love's only a cure until it becomes a regret.
but you could've just left a note when you
decided to break my heart.
i don't know why the fish had to die too.

black friday.

there's a hill behind my parents' house
and every year we climb about halfway
light a joint
and watch my mother
grease up a turkey through
the kitchen window.

the trail home used to be silent.
across the meadowlands,
down the turnpike,
but it's never cold anymore.
nothing crawls underground
or goes inside.
the ride gets longer each year.
i don't smile much now.
i don't want to thank my country.
my grandfather came back with
shrapnel in his cheek and
no cartilage in his knee.
my dad can't breathe and he pretends
his friends aren't paved beneath
the new shopping mall
in the freedom tower.
i think i've been failed too.
eighty years ago in russia
they spread butter on their boots
and ate their dogs
and never had to lower their flag as the nazis
pointed guns at stalingrad.

i've never fought for anything
and usually
my father coughs and yells at me
for sleeping too late.
but it's black friday,
they're all out shopping,
and the house is quiet
until the dogs wake up
from the neighbors laughing
and hanging christmas lights
next door.

everyone hates a person who looks at children
like rats playing in the snow
and the coffee is never close
when you stare out the window
and ask the dogs,
"what do they know?"
and
"why don't they want to die
like i do?"

II.

hollywood hell

(written in los angeles, california late 2016)

my suitcase is packed.

i know you're home somewhere out there
in colorado
where the desert flowers
wait all year to turn yellow
and horses with spanish blood
whip their manes under lightning
as the snows melt down to refill
dried beds.
somewhere where enough was enough
and you had to put a continent between me
and new jersey.
i've seen that land and pulled over
to swim naked
where the white crests shatter
and freedom is something more
than a dream.
there are no dead ends on your streets,
the rain only falls straight down
and even stray cats
come when they're called.
i bled for you once
when the war was still far from over
and the end hasn't gotten any closer
so i guess
i'd do it again.

new friends.

we saw the end of the sun some time ago
and i thought about california
and the palm trees that were still eating
and the girls in the sand
and their hair in the wind
and how it didn't matter to me anymore
where the lightning bugs went
once the days cooled off,
or why old men never died like outlaws
if it's what we all want.
born alone.
legacy always in question.
life has a way of herding the useless together,
drafting us into a showdown
that began
long before the dead had to
explain their worth.
bellies up.
no closure.
no kind words left behind
for the kids.
we forgot a long time ago that
the world will keep rolling over
like it always has.
so we laugh at the snoring dogs
shaking their jaws
and running in place,
but now i wonder:
why are they the only ones

who sleep deeply enough
to dream?

i'd been locked up at my
girlfriend's parents' house for a week
and all anyone could talk about
was a skunk that lived in the woods.
and every night i'd go outside
and stare into the trees
but i never saw anything.
the sun dropped,
the geese flew south,
and just as i was about to give up
for the last time
a little skunk crawled out from
under the shed.
i jumped up and waved at him
and he looked back as friendly
as any fat and free thing
and neither of us did much more
than that.
but then my girlfriend came
out and screamed.
the skunk looked back like i'd
betrayed him,
and as i watched his tail go up
i felt like i'd broken our bond too.
i knew my girlfriend would get mad if
i said it was her fault
so i cursed at the skunk
cursed at the trees

cursed my name
(never going for the one who deserved it),
hating everyone and everything
in this whole stupid world.

her mother made lasagna that night.
i left a plate out by the backdoor.

goodnight moon.

the kids read *goodnight moon* to mom
before they went to sleep
and after the final goodnight
mom realized the children's book
she'd spent a year writing
would never be that good.
was her ex right? was she stupid?

the next morning she poured milk into
the kids' bowls of frosted flakes
and loaded up the minivan.
after the last one was dropped off for homeroom
mom waved at the crossing guard
and parked the car.
then she walked to the pitcher's mound
and lit herself on fire
(with a whole red box of diesel fuel
and a cigarette).
she went up like a wood barn
but they dragged her off in time
and now the other mothers
cup their hands together at her front door
and they share the blue pills
prescribed by dr. patel.

the kids got taken away and mom started
working on a novel.
she never wore a bra anymore
and she traded the minivan

for a mini cooper.
"do you miss the kids?" her friend asked.
mom took the orange pill bottle
between her index and thumb
and shook the pills back and forth
like a macarena.
"not if i have enough of these," she said.

they both laughed and tapped their
pills together with a "cheers".
her ex was wrong.
mom wasn't stupid,
she'd just buried her spark
until it became a volcano.

the santa fe trail.

you can read maps by starlight
in places i've been
and you sleep like shit off the mexican beer
and wake up covered in bites
in hotels where life is impossible
and anything still breathing
wants blood.
did you know what you wanted
at the taco truck in dalhart?
do you know that there's a
whole country out there
that doesn't care about new york?
i do now.
i might know everything now.
i've drank from the shallow creeks.
i've chewed the taco rellenos with
fire still in the seeds.
i looked up for god and every grackle
in the tree followed my gaze.
next time i'll follow the trails in the sand
and the small streams will lead me to the
window rock.
or maybe the other way -
to lie down in a graveyard
where desert rats use cow skulls as ashtrays.
and if the rains ever come again
maybe white petals
will bud up from my bones

and a lost rabbit can
spend a day
sleeping under my shade.

what's enough?

it ends just like it begins.
with us not touching
not talking
not friends.
i would've stayed unhappy with you
for a lifetime
but how many futures
can be built on yesterday?
and can we even fight this familiar hell
if it's better
than lonely?
you told me it could be like
all those mornings
before this
but you forgot
i wake up earlier than you;
i can see it's not me
you're talking to
in your dreams.

and if these brains and hearts
don't ever align
maybe the point *is*
to destroy.
if love never meant
the same thing to anyone
where did we think this would end?
all that truth and rosé
and the promises we made;

the luck finally gives up
but the feelings never do.

let's go on one last date.
follow me
past the boardwalk
to the rocky shore.
and bring that typewriter you bought
at the brooklyn street fair.
we can put our hearts on paper
and stuff them in a bottle,
throw it at the seagulls
and watch our words recede
in the endless tide.
they'll fade off like a memory
that started out so vivid
but years later
became impossible to define.
what else could it be?
i guess with all this emptiness
there's always a little space left
to fill up.
isn't that good enough?

my 30th birthday.

i drank a good scotch all night
from the bottle on the tv stand
i had been saving
for my birthday.
for twenty-nine years my father
hadn't gotten me a thing
but this birthday
he handed me the bottle
and said, "you made it to thirty,
my job's done."

but i didn't think
of my father as i drank.
i thought of her
way up there in harlem
wearing new dresses
and walking new streets,
getting off work each
day and taking home
a new subway.
i thought of how
she got high and didn't say much,
and i'd yell about
the government
or reptilians
and in her silence
i found something to fight.
things like that
used to matter

though i couldn't remember why.
even if i never had to worry about her,
where she was
and who
she'd gone there with.
that didn't seem like enough then,
but it does now.

i was drunk and hungry
and thought of food
my new home didn't have.
and how we
used to walk through the village
for coffee on the way
to vietnamese kitchens
and sometimes see
patti smith on her stoop
or rare breeds of
hunting dogs in the park.
i remembered her feet didn't
reach the ground if she
sat against the back of the bench
and she crossed them at the ankles
and swung them like
a kid on a swing,
like a kid who still knew
there was all the time
left in the world
and nothing was ever
going to go wrong.

there were many days like that.
and some weren't like that at all.

III.

contributions to delinquency

(written in asbury park, new jersey early 2017)

the end of the night.

i remember some good years.
the old pilings of
the baltimore pier
that swayed under the crowd while
we watched our favorite band.
and when i told her
i didn't love her
for the third time
she threw their record at me
and it hurt
but we laughed
until
i decided to break her heart again.

there was the year
i ate sixty oysters
at the aqua grill.
she'd paid attention
when i said
i only wanted to eat oysters
from states i hadn't been to
so she had the maître d'
bring out a special menu
and i tried them all
and the damariscottas
and hog islands were the best.

i woke up in the parking lot
of a long island casino

one time
and when i put
two chips
on red
i won $800.
i paid for everything
that weekend
and the four of us walked home
arm in arm
puking in the snow and laughing
like it was our last night
on earth.
we don't call every year but
i still smile when i think about
that birthday
and the best friends
i never see.

some years
i feel like i'm losing.
and there are others where the score
seems to be even.
i've lost cousins
and girlfriends
and a brown dog
with a white cross on her chest.
but there were the other years.
there were friends who
didn't leave me in their wake.
girls who left me believing i wouldn't
always be let down.

and my mother,
using expensive ingredients
to cook me a birthday dinner
that fit with my new diet,
always making sure something was safe
in a world that started licking its teeth
as soon as you
walked out the door.

tomorrow doesn't always come with a nightmare.
seeds grow.
leaves fall.
i tell my friends to hold up their bottles
and look around.
"remember our tribe," i say.
"nothing will ever be better than this."
and i know i'm right
because i still haven't found a place safer
than a backyard
in new jersey.
and no matter how long i've been gone
there's always a family waiting for me
when i come home.

we're halfway there.

they promised me it was over
but it never ended
it just got worse.
and the shifts grew longer
and the aliens flew away
and the u-boats swam home
and nothing good ever happened.
the chickens got fat
and america dropped the blinds on the nightmare
plaguing everyone
who never made it off the sacred rock.
the one all great-greats sailed here from
when the sun still set
on another empire.
and the lucky ones learned
you don't look back
when it's all on the line,
you buy a happy meal
and drive to death
in a 99' toyota camry
while singing the chorus of
livin' on a prayer.

the blood moons.

she lived in one of those tenements
on rivington
with the straight up staircases
and hallways full of chinese women
bathing their kids
in mop buckets.
it was pretty deep into the lower east side
and maybe it's changed now
but back then it was
one of the last corners
in manhattan where you
could still find a problem.
if i went by late
she was usually too high
to hear the doorbell
so i'd press every button
until i annoyed someone else enough
to buzz me in.

she was one of my favorites
and had just slept with
her second man.
she was excited in a way
that you grow out of eventually,
after enough men
or women
and lies
and neighbors calling the cops
finally leaves you

with nothing
to call new.
her apartment was cold
but the excitement
came off of her
like heat
from the dusty vents.
and i wanted to warn her
not to go all in
but i didn't
because
they'd told me the same
and i never listened.

i felt everything.

the times said there would be
a rare blood moon that night
so we drank on her roof
and played a card game called durak
while we waited for the moon
to bleed.
the clouds came slowly at first
then all at once
and eventually
we hugged
and i just went home.

i saw her the next day and the guy
hadn't called.
the day after either.

she'd saved most of herself
and like a shopper
he'd browsed
and maybe because they're usually pretty easy
he'd bruised
and returned.
she'd listened to everyone else
when they said
"give him a chance"
and i'd heard them
but didn't offer anything.
sometimes it's better
to let them smile for a minute
before they
walk off the plank.

the blood moon fell on her birthday
the next year.
there hadn't been any more men.
she came alone to the bar
and left early,
going home to watch
her favorite movie.
she had learned enough to know
what would
and wouldn't be there for her.

you'll be afraid
until the pain comes.
you'll be in pain
until the anger comes.

and then you'll be just like
the rest of us
and
move on.

beautiful things.

there are beautiful things tucked into your bed
and late some nights
i would watch you lie there
and smile in your sleep.
a happiness i never knew.
and i thought maybe
if i stayed with you awhile
you could show me how that felt.
i was a wet cigarette,
i was a dog you brought in from the cold,
and i stopped thinking about death so much
once i found something
worth the epilogue.
writing is never easy
but it stops
when you're in love.
that endlessness
you were always trying to conquer
is suddenly too small.
it's a foreign country
but a language you speak,
and all the words in all the notebooks
read like they were written for one girl.
so keep your eyes closed
and keep smiling
like we're owed this world.
there was a whole universe once
outside your room
but my memory

is gone.
i can't remember anything else
i was ever searching for.

night before thanksgiving.

i can't help thinking about it now.
i know you're back
in our hometown tonight.
at the irish bar or your parents' backyard.
surrounded by ex-boyfriends
and some
that never got so lucky.
please don't dance with them.
don't say you'll be right back
and wait in the bathroom line
while they try and figure out an angle.
and since you never liked clever men
the drinks come free with your smile.
you can play the ingénue for
a few rounds
but they know what it means.
no one changes that much
and you always paid back chivalry.

do you still see music?
i hear those songs
sometimes
on moonlit drives
and i press the pedal until the checkers
in the street become straight lines.
like a sailor following a dove back to galilee,
but at the end of the road
the music ends
the memories begin

and all i've done
is follow some tail lights
in new jersey.

jersey shore.

there you were
on that jersey sand
in a white bikini
like marilyn monroe
pinned up on a teenager's wall
or in a jail cell
over a fresh coat of paint.
a girl from a different era
when everything was good
and no sea turtles
swallowed six-pack rings
and i could take my baby
down the parkway
to the casino lights
on a saturday night.

you'd heard about me
but we were kings and queens
so i asked you out anyway.
and you looked back at your friends'
shaking heads
and saw that they cared about your sanity
not your happiness
so you said yes.
i knew forever
could start like that
so i made a mixtape for the drive
and picked you up at seven.

you were a dream i'd been saving
since my first life
and your mother
saw it on my face when
she answered the doorbell,
so she sent you out
into a stranger's arms
and didn't worry like she used to.

i remember your high score at the arcade
and the four free pinballs
that dropped in
when you broke the last record.
there wasn't much you were bad at -
at least i can't remember anything now -
and how about that sunrise
over the asbury waves
when we bummed a cigarette
and squinted our eyes into darkness
while the sun took the night
and gave us back our youth?

you told your friends about
every other night.
i'll bet they never heard of that one.

IV.

shaman haman

(written in havana, cuba summer 2017)

a poem for satine: a good boxer.

we started off as strangers,
you and i.
and i'll always wonder,
if there had been others
would i have picked you?
your brothers were already gone
by the time i got there
so i paid for you,
and i didn't realize
until you licked me in the car
how long i'd gone without you,
and how much my corner of this brutal world
needed you.
it was the first time i saw my soul
in something else's eyes.
so we went home
and we built a life.

you weren't like other dogs.
i didn't have to put you on a leash
for our walks.
i just explained trust once
and you never left my side.
the times i went to work
and said "i'll be right back"
you'd watch me from the window,
and no matter how late the shift ended
i never walked back into the house

without your big drooling smile
waiting for me behind the door.

it wasn't always so good, though.
you moved in with my wife and i
during the bad times.
and when the screams turned to fists
i'd watch your ears tuck back
as you ran off to hide.
little whines would float in from another room,
like a child who thought it was their fault,
and i'd spend those nights reminding you
that we'd been best friends in another life,
and that no matter what,
when it came to us,
everything would always be all right.

and it was all right.
i threw tennis balls for you in fields so green
you looked like a deer
lunging through the weeds.
you swam with me in oceans
and walked long hikes,
and even when i forgot a tennis ball
somehow they would appear.
i think that's why i thought you would live
forever.
something always seemed to be
looking out for you.

that's why i made my biggest mistake.

i left you home while i moved on.
i thought i could get a job and
buy you a house with a big backyard.
i went up to maine
even though i saw you growing old.
but i thought love was stronger than time.
i thought i could cheat the universe.
i didn't know
i was rolling loaded dice.
why else would there be a place like maine?
it was made for good dogs
who never ran away.

my parents could hear how much i missed you
so they brought you up for a visit.
and as we crossed the bridge
in that oyster town
your heart gave out.
you fell to the street
and i caught you in my arms.
i pet your soft fur
and pressed my mouth against yours.
and i almost went blind
trying to blow out every ounce of air
i had in my lungs.

i held your body in the backseat
while my dad drove us down to new jersey.
it was too late to dig a grave
when we got home
so i slept with you outside

on the lawn.
and when morning came
the birds didn't sing
and the coffee wasn't strong,
and my dad and i took turns
digging up the earth
before we gave you to the ground.
our hands went up to our heads
and we saluted you like a soldier,
like a best friend,
like something that had brought more happiness
into our lives
than anything before you ever did,
or anything after you
ever could.

but fear has replaced sadness.
you were too good of a dog.
i wonder all the time about where you are now.
are you another dog?
i saw one that looked like you in the park
and followed it home.
what if you were picked up by someone
with no tennis balls?
what if they didn't have a couch
for you to sleep on?

and so i pray now
and i hope
that there is a god.
and i hope he's got a couch

for all good dogs.
i'd empty my bank account
for another minute with satine.
i'd trade years of my life
if i could just tell her "it's okay".
and if i could go back again
i'd take all those hours
i wasted
working for nothing
and learn the ancient bagpipe psalms,
so i could send my friend off like
the hero she was.
another one
death took
way before their time.
another one
i still salute
on late nights
under bar lights.

and if you're there god
please never get annoyed.
please throw her tennis balls
and tell her she's a good dog.
and when you're watching a movie
please drop extra popcorn.
please let her sleep in your bed at night.
and if there's thunder in heaven
please scratch her ears and tell her
 "it'll be all right".

when i look to the west.

she was a baby when they found her
locked up in a room with no mother
and she couldn't sit down
without crying
because a rash had grown
from her three-week-worn diaper.
no one knew her name
and the state didn't want her
so the cops sold her
to the whitest looking family
in the projects
with no papers.
her new parents kept her away
from the other kids
and when she got older
she'd beg her teachers for detention
so she could sit next to someone
and pretend
she had a friend.

and i guess it never got much better.

but she wrote a song about rainbow road.
and the whiskey
tasted pretty good in soda.
and i never sent the calls to voicemail
when she stuck her thumb out
and hitchhiked
somewhere warmer.

i knew she'd make it through those cities
between new york
and california
because
money is easy to come by
when you never knew your mother
or your father.

the postcard came stamped from arizona.
it said: *i'll see the ocean tomorrow,
let's walk in together.*

fun time america.

fascism came to america
in every cheeseburger
served at my parents' barbecue,
swallowed by the fat mouths
of ugly kids
and men in mets t-shirts
and hats that said "life is good" or
"blue lives matter".
and they all bragged about
world war II while the flame flickered out
and no one could explain to them
that the enemy hadn't even
knocked at their door this time,
it was already in their bed.
and they all showed up on main street
to salute the parade this july
because they knew the flag
only flew for them now,
and the rest of us
were just guests
long ago
uninvited.

2nd grade.

the carnival rolled through town
and he saw the gorilla
with a chain around its neck
and the clowns that got no laughs
and it was his father's weekend to have him
so he got extra popcorn
and the $5 voucher
to ride the donkey around the stable.

his father stole him that night
and he watched the exit home
pass by his window
but he didn't say, "take me back".
we'd read about lake erie
that week in school
and he dreamed of eating
hot dogs in cleveland
with sour cream instead of ketchup
and getting so full
that when he lay on his back
seagulls would land on his stomach
and what a great picture that would make.

but the car didn't drive west.
they refueled in suffern
and stayed at a knights inn
behind downtown syracuse.
his father only had enough for one bed

so he gave his son a pillow
and a towel
and made him sleep next to the radiator.
it leaked all night
and the next morning
when they tried crossing into canada
he watched the police point guns
at his father's head
and drag him out of the car.

the whole thing happened
in about forty-two hours
but it had already made the newspaper
and everyone in town was whispering
that they'd both been murdered.
he was back in class by tuesday
and told us that upstate
they advertised naked girls on bright billboards
and he was pretty sure
he'd heard someone say
there was no such thing as santa clause
and we all nodded as we realized
it was over.

that first letdown felt like the bottom.
we didn't know there would be many more.
and they would all be caused by people
we said we loved.
and they would all be worse.

the dream is over pt. I.

it was all good once.
football games on friday nights
and maybe second base
under the bleachers
before the last call cigarettes
and coffee
at the red oak diner.
the future american heroes saved up
for monday morning war stories
and the lucky ones
got fist pounds and made bets on what
was next.
but the stars fell close.
and the good ones got out.
and those years
that once felt endless
didn't prepare us
for a future alone.

the dream is over pt. II.

it was so easy once.
i never had to hunch over the keys
to pull something out.
words just appeared
and the second hand clicked
as i lay on my back
and put onto paper
any good word that came through.
like throwing darts at a wall,
like playing william tell,
and if you do that long enough
no matter how bad it starts
eventually you hit a bullseye.

but they don't come so easy now.
you see, love lived here once,
in these keys,
on that paper,
in the dark corners of the classroom
i faded into as the stories
rolled out from the weekend.
your phone number on a matchbook.
a dinner at the sweet shop of
cherry cokes and disco fries.

the rain fell like blue yarn that fall
and the sun never felt good either.
i wrote you a poem
about an umbrella i had

whose stem was carved into a duck head.
but it was homecoming weekend.
the game sold out.
and they raffled off a new bicycle at half-time
while the sophomores took turns under the
bleachers.

the rain turned to ice on saturday.
my priest sang a homily on sunday.

then it was monday again.

i listened in homeroom while horrible lips
still smiled from the weekend.

you took a vow of silence.
too bad they never did.

V.

bite the dirt

(written in new york, new york 2017)

the experiment failed.

they want their painters dead
their writers dead
their rock stars dead
their emotions
their politicians
their heroes
their children,
   everyone but the police
   and their priests,
they want them dead.
and they'll kill right in the living room
if someone says
it'll help them
get on with their living.
anything to fix a bad morning
and a sleepless night.
as long as it's the same as yesterday
and the super bowl
doesn't take too many
commercial breaks
i guess it can be a good life,
always cheering for someone
and never cheered for
by anyone.

i was pretty angry yesterday
so i took a train up the hudson
to jim carroll's grave
and told him about

my friend in texas
who sits by the highway
and watches mexicans
fight roosters in a dirt lot
behind the wal-mart.
and the one
always drunk and alone
on a harlem fire escape,
waiting for clear nights
to count the tug boats
breaking the current
on their way north.
the poets no one
threw money at
when the words were good
and their guns were loaded
for a third act
that never came.

the radio said art was dead
and the professors ran to cash their checks
before the students realized
their mics had never been plugged in.
and my friends apologized to trees
whose legacies had been robbed
by so many talkers
with so few words.
because nobody wants the truth -
the babies shivering in cold apartments.
the old eating cat food so they
can afford their rent.

no one wants to know life.
no one wants to stand in an elevator
alone with themselves.
haven't we learned they'll go broke
for a minute of hope?
they'll pay extra for happiness.
they'll pay extra to smile at a coffee mug.

there's no credit limit on
the happy ending
and all the rich poets
know it.

casino de montreal.

cashed out
in the backseat
with $2 in quarters
for a slot machine
at the montreal casino.
just past the freezing line
and the last american gas station
where latchkey kids
raid dumpsters for old porn
long before their parents
stop buying them pizza
for finishing a novel.

i won $100 on the first pull
and went outside to call my mom
and tell her
i had just failed out of school.
a black guy followed me
and asked for a cigarette
and when i said no
he put a knife to my throat.
i held my hands up
and faster than i had pulled the lever
he emptied my pockets.

i slept facedown on the carpet
of a chinatown motel for two days
but eventually
i had to eat.

i called my mom and told her
i was broke again,
only this time
it was on a snowbound highway
with no continental breakfast
just outside of montreal.
i thought it was the good kind of failure
but she didn't agree.

it's hard to be man alive,
full of everything but food,
expecting nothing
but sympathy.

green-eyed ashkenazi girl.

little girl,
cold in your classroom
with a tissue in your nose
and sleeping on your shoulders
a yellowed blanket
your grandmother took
from the last shtetl in poland.
the family name carried west
and survived under the wool
while they burned the village and beat the
goats with sticks and rocks.
their screams went for days
over hills
and locked between
the shelves of deep valleys
while god didn't come.
and the past held like handcuffs to dirt
many boots walked above
and nothing survived.
no pictures.
no glory.
just that blanket
yellowed
by time and tears,
sleeping on your shoulders
and tickling your hair
like the chills from a home movie
that took a brief instant of hope
and lifted the veils to forever.

just like w. 3rd at midnight.

i can get through the day
feeling lonely or nothing at all.
but lately
i've been standing on my fire escape -
watching a dog who can't catch its tail -
wondering why
nothing
underneath me
is beautiful anymore.
where's the small girl with spring freckles
who smiles at funerals?
with eyes like subway lights
that crawl around corners
long before the train arrives?
don't i have enough left
to lose a little more?

it can be you.
the girl from oslo or rome
waking up alone right now.
is your ashtray still smoking?
do you have a story you wrote at sixteen
when your notebook
was covered in stars
and all of our parents
were going to stay married?
i'll bet those pages were the same as mine.
was it hard for you like it was for me
when you lost the handle

but time kept moving?
and do you
feel the same as me
when you look to the west?
did the boys of your hometown give
you a chance?
did they ask about your rising sign
or the things your hair does
under the streetlights?
i'm jealous of that first face
and the lips you lost
forever on.
that's the victory for some
but i promise it was never mine.

what if we sailed to the coast
of my ancestors
and let today be just like yesterday?
would you want to share a lifetime of nothing?
just a white room
and an old dog
or a beach with no trap doors
where i can be held with no fear
and give you
everything
that still lives in me.

it takes me longer to get
where the rest seem to start
but that's not
your problem.

i've seen your fawned eyes glow
under every moon
so keep your hair long
and i'll push it behind your ears.
and maybe in the morning
i can name your belly button
and we'll smile
like it's the first time
every time.

just turn the record over before
we say goodnight.
i want to hear you sing some more.

heroes.

they talk a lot about heroes now
because the world has none.
the kids can't go to bed
without kissing the tv goodnight
and after the first mistake
and two marriage-savers are tucked in
mom stays up five extra minutes
to thank jesus. she lifts the blanket
and dad's fart from earlier
is finally free. he's asleep and she thinks
about how easy it would be to put a
screwdriver through his neck.

she takes an ambien from the drawer
and hopes for a good night's sleep.
warm thoughts of murder and
petting zoos take over.
but she wakes up early anyway and
drives to the gym for yoga at sunrise.
why did she marry riley
instead of going to that retreat in taos?

she asks herself this in a parking lot
until her friends catch up
for brunch. for eggs and vodka. to
show pictures of their kids and complain
about the refugee problem.
like we don't all die in the same twilight.
these parades of marching bands

and zeppoles,
where do they go
once sixth avenue ends?
home?
to staten island?
when did they become mothers
who strap their babies in and drive
silver minivans to the petting zoo?
who save quarters all week for
the cereal machine
so the zebras can eat breakfast?

the days roll by like slow tumbleweeds now.
they remember what it was like
to live in the city.
subways always late.
trenches surrounding the boroughs
like an aquarium of old condoms
sturgeon confuse for jellyfish.

but they can afford the vacation upstate.
and every summer they rent a house.
and they can see the town
crying more each year.
they sell booze now where
the sneaker store was.
raccoons roam the park.
the kids can't run through the forest this summer
because the bees never found the flowers.
and it'll always be like that.
the happy days were here once,

but not now.
they were the last generation
to write history books full of heroes.
but they didn't save us.
and the kids get detention
if they talk about them
anymore.

first hit.

i saw the spotlight last night
under the hotel pennsylvania.
he came to new york
like everyone else
and in a city that always played favorites
the pigeons and avenues never turned against him.
the stages warmed up under his feet
and queens
became manhattan
and the kids lined up outside the theater
and whispered to each other
"i've seen him on the subway"
and
"his poster is hanging under the fridays
in times square".

and his parents could finally call their friends.
and their friends could tell their kids
they'd seen a star grow
before their own eyes.
and their smiles lit the heartland
for a night
because everyone knew
that the dream came true
for somebody,
and a win for one
sometimes seems like a victory
for all.

and after the show
we talked about those nights
we'd spent in empty long island city
clapping
and telling our friend that
he had *it*
and someday all the idiots
would see it too.

we raised our pints
and gave him a cheers
(and he smiled his new network grin)
but when the bill came
he asked for a separate check.
and all of us who had to wake up at 7 a.m.
realized
that loyalty is taken for granted,
but when the bill comes
you're always on your own.

your bottom line.

you don't realize how fast this all goes away
the rent
the girls
the cigarettes
your favorite waitress at the boxcar diner
your father who never said i love you
the twin towers
oysters
respect
1 a.m.
a fresh bottle
a new bag
you blink and it's never there again.
and you'll stare as the rent goes up
and the same crackhead sleeps on your stoop
barefoot
in winter. summer.
and the bodega becomes a yoga studio
and the hasidics count the white people
moving into your building
and your mother calls and asks you what's wrong
and you say "i don't know".

you don't know.

it disappears right in front of your eyes.
someone wrote this language to
make sense of what we all see,
but you don't have to explain a nightmare

to know why your teeth grind
in your sleep.
words are just a decoration for life
and i haven't found any yet
to explain what's wrong
to explain complete madness
to explain these years.

but the bum sleeps
and the towers fell
and the cop lights race down broadway
and fade
through my apartment
like a party i wasn't invited to.

#occupy.

i spent a night in the tombs once
down there at the edge
of chinatown.
the world economy had just collapsed
and only ten-thousand college kids
in lower manhattan
seemed to give a shit.

we pitched a tent city in zuccotti park
and the news ignored us
until the old mayor went on tv and
started calling it woodstock.
he meant it as an insult but he
didn't understand his enemy;
we were building the closest thing
to freedom any of us
had ever seen.

a library came first.
then a soup kitchen appeared.
it was going so well
some even said we had brought hope
back to a single square block
under the shadow
of this evil empire.
and we sang songs all day
and made love in tents
all night
while the police lined up

around the perimeter
and called us
"faggots" and "ungrateful".

on my third night
a girl name cecily held my hand
and said, "we're going to take back wall street."
i marched with her down broadway
and as we made a left onto pine
the police formed a barrier.
they slapped bats against their open palms
and the clap built like a war drum
echoing off the old stone.
the meanest cop smiled at us
and said, "lets go, i dare you,"
as the crowd began
to count back from ten.

cecily ran at him
and for five seconds
or five minutes
or five hours
bats and fists swung with
no intention but murder.
and blue blood and red blood
spilled all around me.
i saw cecily fall
but before anyone could get to her
a cop lifted his leg over his gut
and brought his boot down
on the side of her face.

he laughed when she stopped moving.
i think he thought he'd killed her.

the weeks went on like that.
the police would raid the park
and everyone
would run
and when the news showed the videos
the next night at six
america looked at its economy
and didn't care at all
about the sacrifices
its children were making.

just around winter we decided
to close down times square.
the nypd showed up
on horses that time.
they twirled their bats and told us
we had five minutes to leave.
of course nobody moved.
this battle had been brewing for months
and we had walked right in, unarmed.
but this was america, we thought,
the cops wouldn't try and kill their own.
this was america, we thought,
but we were wrong.

the cops pulled back on the reins
and their horses levaded like boxers
toward the crowd.

bodies flew up in the air
and ground down
into the pavement
and our screams drowned the bullhorns
when reality set in -
there were too many of us.
there was nowhere to run.

a net came down over my side of the street.
it trapped about twenty of us
like small bugs in a web.
mace sprayed from all directions
and then a bat blew out
the back of my knee.
the cops beat us for so long
i stopped feeling pain.
i didn't know if my eyes were bleeding
but if i could've lifted my arms
i probably
would've torn them out.
mace is torture.
it hurts much more
than losing faith.

but the next thing i remember was real pain.
they zip-tied our wrists behind our backs
and the nylon cut like the teeth
of a small dog.
my hands turned blue in the back
of the paddy wagon
and the driver hit every pot hole

like our agony was a game.
we begged for the old-fashioned handcuffs
and when a scared kid said
we were zipped too tight
the cops all laughed
and said, "well, you should've thought about that."

on our way to the tombs
i asked the cop driving
about his kids,
about this world we were trying to save
and why
he was dedicated to ruining it.
"my kids will always be taken care of," he said.
i didn't get it then
but he was right.
it came out later that j.p. morgan
had been making weekly donations
to the nypd
since the occupation started.

they cut the zip-ties
when we got to the tombs
and handed us
bologna sandwiches with green meat
and a carton
of blue milk.
i traded my bologna
for cigarettes and stayed thirsty
for fourteen hours.

we sat on broken benches
and tried not to breathe in
the stale shit
someone had left in the only toilet.
every time we started to pass out
an officer ran his bat
against the cell bars.
and just as we thought
it couldn't get any worse
the cops threw a giant in with us
who was high
on pcp.
he swung around the bars
and screamed about aliens
and when we all huddled in the corner
he blew snot
into his palm
and threw it at us.

eventually the doors opened
and the cops
told us to go home.
no charge,
no apology,
just a lesson about
what happens
when you want change
in a free country.

cecily was put on trial a few months later.
it came out that the cops

had punched her
until she went into a seizure
and while she was handcuffed
they molested her
and took pictures.
this is all true.
they're on the internet if you don't believe me.
but the judge was a good boy,
he didn't let the evidence
against the nypd
into the court room.

cecily went off to rikers with a felony
and america slept soundly
for it's 236th year.
and the middle class
didn't ask any more questions
until a nazi ran over a girl named heather
while the president played golf.
"what have we become?" they asked.
after all, we had won world war II,
weren't we the good guys?
but the ones who knew
didn't see a reason to answer.
the suburbs don't want to hear
about too late,
or a trigger their fingers
will never touch.

VI.

yeti funeral

(written in prague, czech republic early 2018)

a place for everyone.

do you remember the first time?
i went to the place where
all the lost wishes go that lovers
make on stars
but never hit their mark.
a place beyond the sun
that died long before
the first man
loved the first woman.
and if time traveled as fast
as youth
as loss
as regret
we wouldn't have to spend
so much of it looking back.
we could stand on each other
like a pyramid of hearts,
one beating love that
could never break,
or a hive that moves
the stragglers along
so no one is left.
because that blue that we stare at
that turns into black
has been there for years
and switches like the channels
on a television set.
so don't worry,
i won't bury you when you're gone.

i'll climb the mountain and lie down
on the rocks.
i'll stare up at the space beyond the sun,
that place they say no one has been
but we both know they're wrong.
every smile, every tree
has some remnant of a god.
and we know that place
they come from
belongs to everyone.

someday i'll get this right.

were you wired wrong for this
kind of love?
to wait tables
spend your tips on wine
a new haircut
and a doormat for
me to come in and
stomp my boots?
let the gray and polluted
new york snow melt in.
listen to me complain about the city.
and if you're lucky
i'll say, "i'm happy to see you."
or, on really dark nights,
i'll tell you how beautiful you are,
the only thing to blossom
while the rest of the world
has been dying.

were you wired wrong
for this kind of love?
the one where i push you out
then drag you back?
go home to my parents' house
and pretend
nothing happened?
i guess we know you won't
put up any argument.
and i guess you know

i'll expect no consequence.
i never thought about you
moving on.
and i liked it better
when i had no hope.
these choices they talk about
don't seem so optional
when we make them
against a wall.
the first verse leads to a chorus
and everyone sings along.
but by verse two it's boring.
and by three the audience
just wants to go home.

this love wasn't a total waste, though.
at least i taught you about forever.
you don't stand under the stars anymore
and pretend they're alive.
it just seems that way
because they die slower
than love.

lucky us.

i knew love once.
it was back before
my first execution.
before the hounds were released
and the hunt was easy for fresh blood.
back when i sat on my floor and
pictured a wild west
and if my mom asked me what i was doing
i'd say, "listening to music."
and she'd smile at the simple world
that once spun so slow
an old record could
take up whole nights.

but not now.

not since i opened and closed
and forgot to buy postcards in
havana and minneapolis.
and if i promised to let people know
i was still alive
i didn't remember or worry
because somewhere along the way
i learned
no one really cares.
and the girls don't need
a prince on a horse
by the time they're ready to kiss
their fathers goodbye.

they just want what's there.
and if it hasn't gotten drunk and
beaten them yet
it's worth saving.

inventing a history is easier than thinking about
what might have been.
who needs love anyway?
a new show premieres every night at eight.

fin de ses jours à grand est (6/8/2018).

the moon fled early
and left us dirt-stained
and hungry
halfway between saint marks
and the sushi bar
we drank saki in for your birthday.
where duke got run over
by an off-duty taxi
and laura came late
and found him inside out.
it was a perfect ending.
to die for nothing.
and in the final quiet
someone said
"even flowers grow in the fields of bastogne".
and i never forgot that.
the beautiful order.
and it made sense
until i watched anthony bourdain die
on a tv hanging above
a cold cuts counter
in alphabet city.

we shared my grilled cheese
on the walk home
and laughed about
the worst endings we could imagine.
but his still beat them all.

it held a truth
we couldn't speak.
and the sun didn't clean us again
but we didn't complain that time
because
we'd lost all hope,
and we knew then
that strasbourg
wasn't a fairy tale,
and it was never built to save us.

the clock set back.

the shadows come early as the middle
shifts closer to the sides.
children cup their hands under the blind bird
and their giggles warm the schoolyard
when she drops a worm for fun.
a wet tickle in their palms as it curves down
and nestles into the ravines of their new veins.

so shallow.
so easy to steady.

old night-lights ground the runway
when the triangle calls them home.
no desert in their smiles
walking hand in hand
underneath a scarred and coming moon.
feathers replace the leaves.
old wars still fought.
they don't know yet that all things
can split or shatter
or fray from the seams.
even when mothers stop crying,
and everything once declared empty
fills up.

there's another end to all migrations.
other sidewalks the birds will sing above.
a place water sleeps under bridges and dirt
and cormorants drift with the current

until a fence cuts them off.
the pyramids crumbled to dust
in those backyards
but still
no desolation pales their eyes.
they weren't born from love,
and free of its promise
they can fly from winters
from summers
from shadows and sun.
even at the mercy of the same moon
they'll never be martyrs
of something unsown.

there's an empty branch out there awaiting
a new breeze.
just above the dreaming puppies.
just above the rabbits waiting patiently
for the coming thaw.
plain as the cormorants coat.
plain as the worms digging new tunnels.
plain as the leaves growing brighter dead.

VII.

boondocked in perico

(written in hereford, texas late 2018)

the exodus.

the boats landed in lower manhattan
and unloaded the irish
the germans
terrapin, trachoma, clams,
and whatever else
the old country left alive
to feed the new american dream.

their boots marched on fresh dirt
everyone swore
would stay cleaner on this side.
and the oyster shells crunched
under the cobblestone,
the cathedrals built up along the park,
and those with new names
frowned in chimney ash that
burned the same as back home
but for the first time
blinded hope.
how long could they have stood
on those docks
before they realized
what they had done?

the bronze lady wasn't green yet
and the candles still burned
in the south street beer halls.
horses shit as they marched down the street
while babies waded home

in the warm bath.
and ancient hymns
about a far-away river shannon
broke the heat
as dogs packed the alleys
and waited like panting gargoyles
for spoiled carrots
to roll off the pushcarts.

but the bronze lady greened.
and the boats sailed back.
and no one looked up
at the big men in gold towers
shaking hands with their friends.
the poets wrote home
about a dream that was dead
but
it was never more alive
in america
in germany
in the future brazil.
the poor were always sliding
down the mountain,
they just found a new country
where they believed
lies could come true.

the throne.

i don't want them to have hope
i know what they'll do with it.
it becomes freedom
it becomes equality
it runs away from the founders
and digs deeper trenches.
you've had a best friend,
were they there when you needed them?
everyone's been burned by
the ones they love.
you can hear it in the cop's voice
as he clears the street.
a man with blood in his eyes
a man who doesn't care who pays his checks.
where's the honor in dying for a nation
that forces everyone
to sleep with the lights on?
they know that when the armies retreat
and the dark horse gets the gun
there's never a sanctuary for the guilty.
the streets run back the other way
and finally the underdog
gets the thing he used to pray for.
but the throne was always a funny thing.
all men want it
and no one ever knows
what to do with it.

men.

i never questioned
that my father was a real man.
he could do
those
things -
give a funeral speech
without tears,
build a shed
and fill it
with tools
he knew how
to use -
the things they say
make a man.

he couldn't hear
from the sirens,
and he couldn't
breathe from
the 9/11 smoke,
but the call
sounded and
he rushed in.
"you do your job," he said.
"you go to work everyday
knowing something
like that
will happen."

the things
they say
make
a man.

my father
had no doubt
that i was not a man,
had none of the qualities,
and didn't show
much hope
of figuring it out.

he used to say,
"you think
you just flush a toilet
and it goes away?
what's going to
happen when it doesn't
go away
and it comes back
and you and all your idiot friends
are drowning
in poop?
you're all gonna die
because
you don't even know
how to use a toilet plunger.
you'll see."

his brother was the same.

he wrestled
in high school
and he always said
it taught him things
but
as far as i could tell
he did everything
wrong.

they both had
a favorite place to give advice:
on the couch
during football commercials.

i always found it hard
to concentrate on words
men spoke
while watching
other men
throw balls at each other
and try their hardest
to lie on the most
submissive one.

sports.
this was supposed to be
the triumph
of all men.
and every sunday
my dad would yell
and cry,

never giving any thought
to after the game,
when
all forty of them
took one big shower together.

the forced encore.

you were a kid once
and named songs like
epitaphs because the gun
was always against your head
and the white keys
weren't enough back then.
but the gods are unkind
and the streets crack
from wheels dragging under
old steel.

the crowds count down now
but the fat lady never sings.
there was a poem you
put into every song
about an early death
because
like a warmer winter
or the gideons bible
life rarely seems like a gift.
and when the lights come on
the crowd still has some beer
in their cups.
they paid the cover.
your sweat wasn't enough.

get back out there.
pull the ghosts from the eight-track.
you can sleep tomorrow as the van

pulls headfirst into a sunrise
and somewhere long ago
you might remember a kid
whose only dream was this life.

clayton, nm.

i saw the vfw in downtown clayton
and watched the past lay naked
around an unplugged jukebox
while the first drop of rain in six years
hit the window
just before happy hour.

sad spit
from the big blue monster.
always above.
holding nothing of god.
never smiling at the peasants below
still kneeling on roads
they'd run cattle down
when dew grew the crop
and the rivers
rushed with gold.

luckily i found a $0.50 postcard at goodwill
so i could write home
and tell my mom
that i'd seen the end now -
the scalped heads impaled
on the picket fences,
the weatherproof eviction tags,
and the bagpipes they hadn't even blown
because there was no one left
to hear them.

the greyhounds all drove on to trinidad
and the prairie dogs
looked to the buzzards
and begged them,
"please,
just make it quick."

mercy me.

i can get the rifle loaded
if you want to cook
dinner tonight.
thanks for letting me
hang around this long.
i know i said i'd be gone by winter
but running just doesn't seem
so cool this time.
i'm sure you've heard
but
california's burning again
and i never could decide
on a last meal.
i always liked your cooking though
so just give me
last night's leftovers
and leave them out by the door.
i'll fold my clothes in a nice pile
behind the shed
and when you come outside
i'll help you pop the safety.
don't be scared,
this was always going to be my ending.
i know it's a lot to ask
but there's a dog i want to hold again
and i think next time
i really can do better.
just pull the trigger, my love.

put me down like the sick pony
my life always was.

Made in the USA
Monee, IL
23 August 2020